Viva Mexico!

The Foods

George Ancona

Benchmark Books

MARSHALL CAVENDISH
NEW YORK

To Katharine Kagel

Gracias to the people who helped me with this project:
Gabriel Alatriste Montoto in Puebla,
Chef Manuel Bonnilla S. of Hotel La Rotonda,
Victor *(Chicharo)* Carrasco and his family in Veracruz,
Jim Dunlop of Alla Books,
Katharine Kagel of Cafe Pasqual,
Genoveva Rosales Lopez and her family,
Benjamin and Martha Salazar,
Doña Noemi Santiago in Oaxaca,
Barbara Mauldin of the Museum of International Folk Art.

Benchmark Books
Marshall Cavendish Corporation
99 White Plains Road
Tarrytown, NY 10591-9001
Website: www.marshallcavendish.com
Copyright © 2002 George Ancona

Library of Congress Cataloging-in-Publication Data
Ancona, George.
The foods / by George Ancona.
p.   cm. – (Viva Mexico!)
Includes index.
ISBN 0-7614-1328-6
1. Cookery, Mexican—Juvenile literature. [1. Food habits—Mexico. 2. Cookery,
Mexican.] I. Title. II. Series.
TX716.M4 A63 2001   641.5972—de21   00-053017

Printed in Hong Kong
6 5 4 3 2 1

Contents

A Happy Heart

Panza llena, corazón contento is an old Mexican proverb that means "a full belly makes for a happy heart." The foods of Mexico are a treat to see, smell, taste, and eat.

Like seeds blown by the wind, people came to Mexico from distant lands, and they settled and flowered. The foods they brought with them blended with native cooking. The result is a Mexican cuisine that has traces of distant lands—and makes for a happy heart.

Preparing ingredients for tamales.

***El Mercado* (The Market).**
Mexican cooking begins in the marketplace. Although there are supermarkets in most cities, towns house their markets in large open buildings. In many towns, there is a weekly market day. Farmers and vendors from the region bring their wares to sell. Large sheets of colored plastic are strung over the streets to shade the vendors and their goods. Radios provide background music for the shouts of merchants praising their wares.

From the times of the ancient cities, markets have bustled with people who come to sell and those who come to buy. To wander through a Mexican market is an adventure of colors, sounds, and smells. The stalls are heaped with vegetables, fruits, meats, fish, cheeses, beans, chile peppers, and many other foods from Mexico's earth and waters.

Markets have always brought people and food together. Hungry shoppers and merchants can sit at a food counter to eat a simple taco or a full-course meal.

An early farmer harvests his field of maize.

Native Foods

The First Farmers. About seven thousand years ago people in the Western Hemisphere began to raise their own food. Farming made it possible for villages and cities to expand because people could stay in one place and raise their crops. The early people of Mexico developed maize (corn) from a small wild plant. They grew many varieties of maize: white, red, yellow, black, and other color combinations.

Between rows of corn they planted tomatoes, beans, chiles, pumpkins, sweet potatoes, and squash. They also raised avocados and amaranth, a nutritious grain that was ground into flour for tortillas and bread. Fields and forests supplied fruits, peanuts, cacao (cocoa) beans, honey, and mushrooms. After the spines were removed, the cactus called *nopal* was grilled lightly to make a tasty meal. *Tuna,* the brightly colored cactus fruit, which is sweet and juicy, was also eaten.

Four types of maize

Fishermen and Hunters. Fishermen brought their catch from oceans, rivers, and lakes to the markets. They sold fish, lobsters, shrimp, eels, octopuses, frogs, snails, oysters, clams, crabs, turtles, and snakes.

Hunters sold turkeys, ducks, pheasants, rabbits, opossums, armadillos, tapirs, iguanas, peccaries (wild pigs), and deer. And they also raised chubby dogs to eat. In the ancient marketplaces, people paid for what they bought with cacao beans.

Today many of these foods are still found in markets and served in Mexican homes and restaurants. But nobody eats dogs anymore.

An ancient pottery figure of an itzcuintli, *a dog raised for food*

The Spanish Flavor

The Spanish who came to the New World brought their traditions with them. Over the centuries Spain had had many influences. From the Greeks, who colonized Spain in the fifth century B.C., the Spanish learned to grow olives, grapes, and chickpeas. From the Moors, who ruled their country for eight hundred years, they learned to plant spinach, eggplants, artichokes, watermelons, sugarcane, and lime, lemon, and orange trees.

By the fifteenth century the Spanish had freed themselves from Moorish rule and become great navigators, explorers, and conquerors. Their ships returned from Africa and Asia laden with exotic fruits such as pineapples. Among the many spices they discovered and traded for were saffron, pepper, ginger, cinnamon, cloves, and nutmeg. In 1492 Columbus discovered the Americas. Spanish settlers began to arrive in Mexico, which they called New Spain, and with them they brought their foods and traditions.

BANANAS

PLANTAINS

WATERMELON

PINEAPPLE

SUGAR

CINNAMON

ORANGES

LIMES

PLUMS

RICE

OREGANO

OLIVES

PEPPER

CLOVES

In 1493, when Columbus returned to the New World for the second time, his ships unloaded horses, cattle, goats, sheep, chickens, and pigs. These animals were brought to New Spain, where they flourished and began to change the diet of the Mexicans.

SHEEP

PIG

CATTLE

ROOSTER

Spanish ships called galleons sailed across the Pacific Ocean from Spanish colonies in Asia. They brought many foods and spices with them. Rice from Asia together with Mexico's native beans *(frijoles)* and tortillas became the staple food of Mexico. African slaves who were brought to New Spain also added their ways of cooking.

Foods Today

La Tortilla. The tortilla is a round, flat bread made of maize. In the home, women are usually the cooks. Some grind the corn in the traditional way on a grinding stone called a *metate* to make the dough, or *masa*. Then they shape the tortillas by hand and cook them on a skillet, or *comal*.

In rural areas women take
pride in making tortillas
before each meal. But now
they often take their corn
to a local mill to be ground.
At home they flatten a ball
of dough in a hinged tortilla
press made of metal or wood.

The simplest Mexican meal is a *taco,* food rolled up in a tortilla. Tacos may be filled with cheese, beans, chiles, and different kinds of meat—shredded pork, chicken, or crumbled *chorizo* (Mexican sausage). The tortilla keeps the filling warm, and since you can eat it with your hands, no forks or knives are needed.

Tortillas are made in many sizes and used in different ways. They can be folded, stuffed, pinched, fried, or cut into pieces for chips. Not only is the tortilla the bread of the meal but by tearing it into smaller pieces it can be used to scoop up food. In the state of Oaxaca, people eat huge tortillas called *tlayudas*. An *empanada* is a tortilla, with a filling, that is folded in half, pinched closed, and then cooked.

Tamales. *Tamales* are one of the ancient foods still eaten today. Tortilla dough is spread on a banana leaf or cornhusk. The dough is then filled with meat and sauce, rolled, tied up, and steamed in a large pot. There are also sweet tamales made with fruit fillings. When you eat a tamale, don't forget to remove the outer wrapping to reach the hot and tasty food inside.

Tortillas o Bolillos? **(Tortillas or Rolls?).**
The Spanish planted wheat because they
preferred wheat bread to the native corn
tortillas. They baked little rolls called
bolillos. Serving *bolillos* was a status symbol
among Europeans. But Mexicans never gave
up their tortillas. Eventually the settlers
began to eat them too.

Today it isn't necessary to choose between
a *tamale* or a *bolillo*. You can have both!
Street-corner food vendors sell a breakfast
snack that blends two cultures: a sliced
bolillo with a hot tamale inside. This
is called a *torta de tamale*,
a tamale sandwich.

ANCHO CHILE

MULATO CHILE

ONION

MIRASOL CHILE

GARLIC

PASILLA CHILE

CLOVES

BASIL

CUMIN

PEPPER

TOMATO

CORIANDER

CHOCOLATE

CINNAMON

TORTILLA CHIPS

Mole. During the five hundred years since the arrival of the Spanish, Mexico's cuisine has gradually become a blend of homegrown foods and foods brought from all over the world. The best example is *Mole Poblano,* which is considered its national dish. The name *mole* comes from the word *moler,* to grind. No one knows for sure how it was created. But a story is told about a nun cooking in a convent kitchen during the colonial period. She wanted to make a dish that would combine the foods of the Americas with those of the Old World.

She started by cooking a native turkey. For the sauce she ground together toasted chiles and tomatoes. Then she added Old World spices: cloves, cinnamon, pepper, and sesame seeds. As she cooked and stirred she tasted the sauce. Something was missing. She looked around and saw some pieces of chocolate. By adding chocolate to the chile sauce, *Mole Poblano* was born.

***Chiles en Nogada* (Stuffed Peppers in a Nut Sauce).**
To celebrate Mexico's independence from Spain in 1821,
the nuns of the convent of Santa Monica, in Puebla, created
a dish. They called it *Chiles en Nogada*. It had the three
colors of the flag of the new nation: red, white, and green.
They stuffed green poblano chiles with ground meat mixed
with tomatoes, fruits, raisins, and almonds. They cooked the
chiles in a creamy walnut sauce. Red pomegranate seeds
were sprinkled over the white sauce, and a sprig of parsley
added a touch of bright green.

Let's Eat!

El Desayuno **(Breakfast).** In November 1519, when Spanish conquistador Hernán Cortés arrived in the great city of Tenochtitlán, the king, Moctezuma, greeted him with a bowl of hot chocolate.

Today chocolate is made by mixing sugar, vanilla, and cinnamon with ground cacao beans. To make the drink, pieces of chocolate are broken into a wooden pitcher. Hot milk or water is added and beaten with a wooden paddle called a *molinillo* until the chocolate is frothy. A cup of hot chocolate with *pan dulce,* a sweet bun, and fruit makes a wonderful breakfast.

***El Almuerzo* (Brunch).** Later in the morning, about eleven o'clock, it's time for a heavier breakfast of eggs, meat, tortillas, beans, rice, and vegetables. This brunch is called *el almuerzo.*

An *entomatada* is a tortilla folded twice, fried lightly, and served with a piece of chicken. This is covered with tomato sauce, onions, a stringy white cheese, and parsley. It's delicious!

Since they begin at seven in the morning, factory workers take a mid-morning break to eat an almuerzo *in the cafeteria.*

Rolando digs into his entomatada.

Don *Victor, the grandfather, sits down to share an* almuerzo *with his son, Victor, and his grandson, Victor Adrian.*

La Comida (Dinner). Dinner is typically the day's big meal. At about two o'clock in the afternoon, families gather at home. Children return from school, and parents return from work. They all sit down to eat and talk about the day's events. Afterward, because of the heat, they rest or take a nap called *la siesta*. Around three o'clock, the adults go back to work, and the children go back to school or play.

Today things have changed because people have to travel far to their jobs. Air-conditioned offices and factories make it possible for people to work through the hot days. Since many working people have only half of an hour for lunch, the *comida* is reserved for Sundays.

La Cena (**Supper**). After a big midday dinner, supper is usually a light snack. Friends gather for a taco and a drink then go on to the movies, night school, a sports event, or a stroll in the *zócalo,* the main plaza. Before returning home it is a treat to stop for a dish of ice cream.

There are many flavors of *helados* (ice creams) and *nieves* (sorbets) to choose from. In addition to chocolate and vanilla, there are ice creams made with tropical fruit such as *pitaya*, *tuna*, mango, or caramel, and cinnamon with sugar, to name only a few.

Frutas y Dulces **(Fruits and Sweets).** Fruits are sold in markets and on street corners. In the morning, orange juice is sold to people scurrying off to work. Freshly cut watermelons, mangoes, oranges, papayas, and coconuts are served together as fruit cocktails, blended into smoothies called *licuados* or squeezed for their juices.

Thirsty shoppers buy fruit-flavored
drinks served from large glass crocks.
The vendor ladles the drink into a
plastic bag with a straw. The customer
then strolls off while sipping the drink.
Mexico overflows with tropical fruits.
Among the drink's many flavors are
strawberry, lemon, a drink made of
almonds and melon seeds called
horchata, pineapple, watermelon,
and *tamarindo*.

Mexico is famous for its candies. Most are made of local fruits and vegetables—tamarind, guava, figs, pumpkin, orange, coconut, peanuts, milk, chocolate, pistachio, sweet potatoes, nuts, and limes. The candies' many shapes are decorated with intricate designs. The sweets are sold in the shops that make them. Their mouth-watering window displays are a blaze of color.

Windows show models of the elaborate cakes and pastries the bakers prepare for weddings, birthdays, and *quinceañeras,* celebrations of girls' fifteenth birthdays.

The Rosales family gathers around their rosca.

Fiestas

La Rosca. Many holidays are celebrated with special meals.
Children receive gifts on January 6, Three Kings Day, instead
of on Christmas. This was the day the kings arrived in
Bethlehem, bearing gifts for the newborn Jesus.

    On this day a large, ring-shaped pastry or cake called *la Rosca
de Reyes* (King's Day Cake), is baked. It is shaped like a crown
and decorated with colorful dried fruit to look like jewels.
Inside the sweet pastry is a little china doll,
el Niñito, which represents the baby Jesus.
If the piece of rosca that you cut contains the
little doll, your parents must host a feast of
tamales the following month on
La Candelaria, The Holiday of Candles.

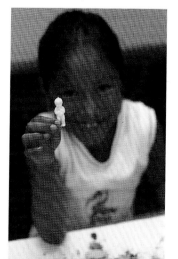

    Montserrat and the Niñito *she found in her* rosca

La Candelaria. On February 2, *La Candelaria,* friends and family reunite to honor *el Niño Santo,* a doll of Jesus as a little boy. The one whose piece of rosca has *el Niñito* is the godfather or godmother of the doll. He or she makes new clothes for the doll and takes it to church to be blessed. Afterward, the *tamalada,* the tamale feast, is served. There are five kinds of tamales. Four are filled with different meats and chile or mole sauces, the fifth is filled with fruit. This is a time to relish tamales, to laugh, and to feel *el cariño—* affection for one another.

Daniel makes a funny speech about the tamales.

43

***Buen Provecho!* (Enjoy Your Meal!).** Fiestas are not complete without hours spent at the table, in a dining room or kitchen, on a porch, at a picnic, or even on a boat. Near Mexico City are the floating gardens of *Xochimilco*. This was where the Aztecs raised their crops for the great city of Tenochtitlán (present-day Mexico City).

People gather in the gardens to spend a holiday or to celebrate a birthday or anniversary. Flat-bottomed boats are hired by the hour. Each boat is poled through the canals by a boatman who stands on the stern. Families sit around a table eating the picnics they have brought. They buy hot tortillas from women in tiny boats who make them on their charcoal stoves. The party spends the afternoon eating and singing to the music of *mariachis* (musicians) who float by. As boats pass, happy diners greet each other with a wave and a shout of *Buen Provecho!* a polite way of saying, "Enjoy your meal!"

Guacamole

2 ripe avocados
½ cup diced tomato
½ cup white onion, finely chopped
1 finely chopped chile serrano (optional)
⅓ cup cilantro, coarsely chopped
1 tablespoon fresh squeezed lemon juice
salt to taste

Peel the avocados and discard the pits. With a fork, mash the avocado in a bowl. Mix in all the other ingredients. Use as a dip with tortilla chips or add to tacos. If not served right away, cover the bowl with plastic wrap or foil and refrigerate. (This keeps the guacamole from turning brown.)

Arroz con leche—Rice Pudding

¼ cup rice
½ cup water
1 cup milk
½ cup sugar or honey
2–3 drops of vanilla
1 stick cinnamon
5 to 10 raisins, depending on size

Ask an adult to help you with the stove. Rinse the rice in cold water. Half cook the rice in boiling water, about ten minutes. In a separate pot bring to boil the milk and sugar, the stick of cinnamon, and the vanilla. Strain the water from the rice. Pour the hot milk mixture over the rice and continue cooking the rice until it is tender. If using honey instead of sugar, add it now along with the raisins and stir together. Sprinkle powdered cinnamon on the rice and serve in small bowls. Makes 4 servings.

Glossary

Here are the Spanish words used in this book.

almuerzo: brunch, late breakfast

arroz: rice

bolillo: bread roll

Candelaria: holiday of candles (Candlemas Day)

cena: supper

chile: a kind of pepper

chorizo: Mexican sausage

comal: skillet

comida: midday meal; dinner

frijoles: beans

desayuno: breakfast

empanada: stuffed, folded tortilla (turnover)

entomatado: any food with tomato sauce

guacamole: avocado dip

guanabana: tropical fruit

helado: ice cream

leche: milk

licuado: fruit drink or shake

mercado: market

metate: grinding stone

mole: chile sauce

molinillo: wooden beater

nieve: sherbert

nogada: nut sauce

nopal: cactus

pan dulce: sweet bread

pitaya: tropical fruit

Poblano: coming from Puebla, an early Mexican city and state

Quinceañera: girl's fifteenth birthday

rosca: round holiday cake

siesta: afternoon rest or nap

tamalada: tamale feast

tamale: dough with stuffing, wrapped and cooked in cornhusk or banana leaf

torta: sandwich

tlayuda: large tortilla

tortilla: flat round bread

tuna: cactus fruit

Find out More

Coronado, Rosa. *Cooking the Mexican Way.* Minneapolis: Lerner Publishing Group, 1992.

Dawson, Imogen. *Food & Feasts with the Aztecs.* Parsippany, New Jersey: Silver Burdett Press, 1995.

Illsley, Linda. *Mexico.* New York: Raintree Steck-Vaughn, 1999.

Tabor, Nancy. *El Gusto del Mercado Mexicano: A Taste of the Mexican Market.* Watertown, MA: Charlesbridge Publishing, 1996.

Index

Page numbers in **boldface** are illustrations.

Photo © Helga Von Sydow

About the Author

George Ancona's parents came from Mexico, but he grew up in Brooklyn, New York. He had many friends who loved to come to his house because it was filled with the wonderful smells of his mother's cooking. Everyone was sure to get a taco with a cup of hot chocolate. When he graduated high school he went to Mexico for the first time. There he got to know his extended family. He was always invited to eat regardless of the time of day. He has never stopped visiting Mexico or eating Mexican food.